What She Really Means

and Other Poetry

©2023 Catherine West-McGrath

Published by Parks & Mews 2023

The right of Catherine West-McGrath
as the author of this work
has been asserted by her
in accordance with
the Copyright Designs and Patents Act 1988.
All rights reserved, including
the right of reproduction
in whole or part in any form.

ISBN:978-1-7391133-2-2

Other poetry collections
from Catherine West-McGrath:

Homesick for the North and Other Poetry

Lapsed Capitalist: A Poetry Collection

Optimistic Activist: Poetry and Verse

British Values: A Poetry Collection

Try This, It Might Help: Poetry and Verse

The Poems and Lyrics

Air Mail 1
What She Really Means 2
The Authority Gap 3
Elizabethan Age 4
Carolean Age 5
My Old Man's Privilege* 6
Sense of Self 7
Cavaquinho* 8
Pazo Barrantes Albarino 9
The Industrial Correspondent 10
Where Are You Really From? 11
Guests 12
I Speak for You 13
His and Hers Style 14
The Love Bomb Explodes 15
A Seismic Announcement 16
New Job 17
Exceptional Parades 18
Acting Strange* 19
Sharp End of Capitalism 20
Justice for Janitors 21
Arsonists 22
Contain First Ask Questions Later 24
Don't Blame Us 25
Shares 26
The Wind in Their Hair 27
Entente Cordiale 28
Keep Your Vibration High* 29
HR Meeting 30
Productive 31
The Other Black Door 32

Serious Disruption 33
Feedback 34
A Break in the Law 35
Spinning 36
Advocate Not Required 37
No Idea 38
Darwen Street Plaque 40
What I Wanted* 41
Economic Arguments 42
Before the Morning Light* 43
A Paradigm Spell 44
Targets 45
Agency 46
Ignorance, Overwhelm and
 Arrogance 47
How to Talk to Your Child About
 the Cost-of-Living Crisis 48
Still Standing But Wobbling Pt 2 49
Built on Trust 50
The Alternative Economic
 Advisory Council 51
Courtroom Drama 52
Workplace Politics 53
Psychographics 54
Verify You're Not a Robot 55
Your Story is Your Strength 56
Gendered Emotions 57
When We're Given a Choice 58
Going to Thrive 59
Protest at the Panto 60
Unique is My Path 61
Words in Ink* 62

*Lyrics

Air Mail

Aeroplanes were throwing party streamers across the sky

Cow bells in the valley provided the music

The sunshine warmed my face and I smiled at a lizard

The day before I had been all alone in the world

Today I had received your letter

I caught an eagle

And flew away

What She Really Means

What she really means is
Allow me to explain
Forgive the interruption
Let's try for you again

You need to speak more clearly
And make your presence known
These meetings can go on and
It's hard to speak alone

The Chair here may not notice
A small voice from the back
Your argument at risk from
My neighbourly hijack

Allowed to take the credit
When your idea was sound
Before you spoke I thought of something
So much less profound

The Authority Gap

Giving talks or
At lectures appearing
Knew the audience would
Upon hearing
Take in every last word
Of the speech
They had heard
Such authority was
So endearing

While the other knew
They appeared meeker
With a voice more high pitched
Sounding weaker
Though an expert and wise
Heard the listener's surprise
When they told them
They'd taught
The next speaker

Elizabethan Age

A stoic force
So wise and sage
That fine
Elizabethan Age

A Princess
In a gilded cage
For our
Elizabethan Age

As history turns
Another page
Goodbye
Elizabethan Age

Carolean Age

The Carolean Age begun
A new day with the rising sun
Though still before the era starts
We comfort each with saddened hearts

Born to the sound of muffled chimes
Church bells announce the solemn times
Books filled with love and flowers laid
In honour of the vow she made

We step onto the bridge across
Uncertain at this sudden loss
No more to know her hand to guide
A new Age on the other side

My Old Man's Privilege

I want some o' my
Old Man's privilege x 4

I try to get a raise
The boss says 'no can do'
My man goes after me
He's raised a grand or two
Though I got my exams
And work so hard each day
Wonder what I should do
To get me higher pay

I want some o' my
Old Man's privilege x 4

I'm walking down the street
I've got to look around
I wonder who's behind
If I should hear a sound
My man walks happily
He'll even cross the park
No need for no curfew
He never fears the dark

I want some o' my
Old Man's privilege x 4

I might find out one day
My body's not my own
Some court expects me to
Be frightened and alone
My man will never start
The journey I must take
My man will never face
The choice I have to make

Sense of Self

A fragile sense
Of self
Creates a need
To seek
The missing
Pieces
In another
To complete

Who among us
Is most likely
To have
Their sense
Of self
Made fragile
In order to
Serve another?

Pushed out
Pulled in
Names removed
Rights to
Ownership
And agency
Still now are
Fought and gained

A fragile sense
Of self
Creates a need
To seek
The missing
Pieces
In another
To complete

Cavaquinho

When the cavaquinho
Starts the dancing in you
And its strings sing to you
From the start
The start
When the room is swaying
All musicians playing
You can really feel it
In your heart
Your heart

I feel the music
Please don't stop the music
Please don't stop the music
In my heart
My heart oh
x 2

Hear the bossa nova
Play over and over
It's a beat that's
Always in style
In style
Such sweet syncopation
Takes me on vacation
To the place which always
Makes me smile
Me smile

The nylon string guitar
Transports from where we are
Into a cool beach bar
Where we chill
We chill
After we've danced all night
And you have held me tight
And promised you will take me
To Brazil
Brazil

Pazo Barrantes Albarino

Pazo Barrantes Albarino
Coudoulet de Beaucastel
Money must be spent in dining
With donors who know us well

Civil servants try to warn us
Such expenses are off plan
Public money must be channelled
From the public where we can

Hoping such exquisite decor
Will distract when all's not right
Still our US friends aren't fooled as
There's no trading deal in sight

The Industrial Correspondent

The industrial correspondent
Took the lift down
As the business correspondent
Took the lift up

Journalists no longer needed
Union leaders on speed dial
Call centre staff didn't organise
They could be easily replaced

Corporate boards' views
Were required in the new age
Strikes were old news
Share price the new headline

There was no more disruption
To be understood
Until someone asked
'Anyone know what's going on?'

Where Are You Really From?

Where are you really from?
I won't be asked today
It's obvious that I'm from here
I won't be made to say

I'm from this land as all will know
My skin assures I'll be
Unquestioned by a stranger
If they may notice me

I'll never have to justify
The journey someone took
So I could stand in front of them
Regardless of my look

I won't be singled out to feel
I may not fit this space
Degrees of separation
Makes one feel out of place

I won't feel under spotlights
Be pressed to satisfy
I won't be asked that question
Don't need a quick reply

No explanation needed
I can relax I know
No one will think I don't belong
A privilege, I know

Guests

She was your guest
You left a blade
Shouldn't expect
Her bed to be made

No handy phrase book
No guide to show
A painted hotel
Of course she should know

But guests can go unrecognised
If too quick they're pathologized
Perhaps the guest's role is to learn
Her hosts don't wish her to return

I Speak for You

I speak for you
Hear your concerns
Know how my words
Makes your rage burn

I practice lines
Rehearsed too well
Means I remember
How to tell

The language chosen
With such care
Intends for you
To be aware

Hope you won't guess
Your 'enemy'
Is more like you
Than you are me

His and Hers Style

Please someone tell me
What he wore today
I can't seem to find
No reporter will say

I like to have knowledge
Of what partners wear
Yet editors seem
Unwilling to share

I know that her gown
Has military style
With a short-netted veil
That report was worthwhile

But alas I don't know
Where his suit was bought
A search on the web
Delivered me naught

If opinions on her
Once required lots of ink
Shouldn't his style now too
Be appraised don't you think?

The Love Bomb Explodes

At the start it was great
Never failed to reply
Was so sweet on the phone
With their loving reply

Sent a gift in the post
With a message to say
Couldn't wait till we pledged
Our forever one day

Felt so low when apart
And they missed me so much
Ached with longing to feel
Their unique special touch

I was grateful to have
Their attention I know
And requests were obliged
As I couldn't say no

When I questioned one thing
Was the day it all stopped
What a blast we all had
When the Love Bomb was dropped

A Seismic Announcement

A seismic announcement
Is fracking back on?
When the last shocking quake
Made us think it was gone

But now there's a rumour
Becoming a roar
That the movement of Earth
Will be felt still once more

But it's miles from their homes
So they won't feel it there
If some wardrobes get smashed
In the North then why care?

The destruction of land
That some county holds dear
Is a good price to pay
When the profits are clear

There'll be no objections
If we make an N-SIP
Don't trust us if we pledge
That was only a blip

Now the protests are back
Fierce and ready to face
Anyone who wants quakes
In this beautiful place

New Job

This hasn't landed well at all
The optics worse we fear
Communication's fallen flat
The message less than clear

The candidate at interview
Presented just okay
Wooden at first with little spark
No better the next day

Assessments in their competence
Just scraping through the test
The scores in their MBTI
Cause for concern at best

Less than a month in their new role
We have to now confess
Probation only started and
Already what a mess

Exceptional Parades

How lucky that we see these sights
On days we can't forget
Nowhere on Earth can match the pomp
Others must feel regret

These rituals in costume
Our standards none can meet
How dull the lives of foreigners
Who look on with defeat

No marking of the seasons
Or cause for celebration
Unfortunate for those outside
This fascinating nation

Our public shows of status
Puts others in the shade
How jealous they must be of our
Exceptional parades

Acting Strange

Someone told me it would take a miracle
There's nothing to be done for you
Someone told me it would take a miracle
The miracle arrived in you

Long ago you held my hand when
No one else seemed to understand when
No one wanted to listen you
Let me speak
Believed that I could be strong when I
Felt too weak

So yes
I followed when you left
So yes
Your going left me bereft
It's not unusual to find
When there is change
It's not unusual you'll find me
Acting strange

You'll find me acting strange
Find me acting strange
x 2

Parts of me were
Left behind in
Darkened rooms and a
Saddened mind when
Others said there's no real chance that
She'll survive
Told me I was gonna make it and
Kept me alive

Sharp End of Capitalism

At the sharp end of our Capitalism
There's a door behind a lock
Where the fragile and the human
Are removed to feel the shock

Where a culture says a person
Who can't do their forty hours
Is detained on wards of coldness
To be mocked by those in power

Decades shouting that this system
Doesn't care but does more harm
Patients hoping sleeping medics
Finally wake to this alarm

Justice for Janitors

Undocumented unorganised
Dispersed in their towers
Paid cents by contractors
Removed from the powers
Controlling conditions
Controlled every hour
Found strength in a union
No longer to cower

From Century City
In downtown LA
Demanded fair working
And a raise in their pay
Demonstrated solidarity
Shouted louder each day
Until owners were hearing
What they had to say

Spread their message across
To the East from the West
Made the case even cleaners
Deserved food and rest
United together
They could face any test
Janitors in the unions
Worker power at its best

For the least well respected
In the corporate food chain
Those who mopped spots and spills
Of the last night's champagne
From a strike to a movement
To a worldwide campaign
Inspire all needing to
Hear their message again

Arsonists

It's the fire brigade calling
To urgently say
Your house is on fire
Put it out straightaway

> I was burning some rubbish
> Didn't think it would catch
> So I threw on more petrol
> With a rag and a match

Well the flames are engulfing
Can't you feel their strong heat?
It's alarming the neighbours
Watching on from the street

> Let's be patient and see
> You're no expert in fire
> See my house is still safe
> In the flames growing higher

But there'll be no house left
If you choose to ignore
Your delay to address
Now the fire's at your door

> Please get out of the way
> Blocking me with your tender
> As I've only moved in
> Yesterday, please remember

Arsonists cont...

It's too late now just look
And the cause we have found
Was your stubborn refusal
While it burnt to the ground

                                            But it wasn't my fault
                                    Neighbours threw fireworks
                                      Don't blame me for the fire
                                        It was their dirty work

Now your fire's spread to homes
All throughout your fair land
What part of 'Don't'
Don't you understand?

Contain First Ask Questions Later

Contain first ask questions later
But the questions never come
Opportunities for healing
Drowned beneath a deafening hum

Of alarms and boots and key turns
Where a girl who needs some care
Is forgotten in a system
Where compassion's all too rare

And the ones who make it out will
Raise their voice requesting change
Face a stonewall of resistance
Personnel are rearranged

When we stay with harmful models
Built on years of disrespect
Of the patients they should care for
Harm is all we can expect

Don't Blame Us

There are reasons behind the fact you are in pain
And we'll say that it's so again and again
It's a line that we use to create immunity
Allows us to act with a certain impunity

Why let a good crisis like this go to waste?
If you think of the things that we've done in bad taste
Can be blamed on another in a far-away land
Pleading policy choices are out of our hands

But if something might change as you hope that it might
Who then next can we blame if you say all's not right?
There's a long list we'll use and we'll tell you it's true
When the next ones to blame are your family and you

Shares

To redistribute wealth to your friends overnight
Is a fair thing to do though you think it's not right
They'll more likely invest in the shares that you own
In effect what you've done is give your mates a loan

Knowing how they invest will fill up your accounts
As you watch families starve on their meagre amounts
It will flow back to you in the end nice and clean
A legit launderette if you get what I mean

The Wind in Their Hair

The liberation of study
The freedom to learn
To love or break up
To travel and earn

Each snip with the scissors
Each strand on the floor
Each tress on the ground
Makes the pile grow some more

Still we watch on in horror
Knowing sisters somewhere
Are still fighting until they'll feel
The wind in their hair

Entente Cordiale

If we're friends with other nations
Who then can we find to blame?
If we thaw our cold war notions
Do we find another game?

If we try to work together
Who's the villain in our plot?
If our talking makes it safer
Are old enemies forgot?

If no longer using scapegoats
As distractions to get by
Will they stop fearing our stories?
Still, there's always some who'll try

Keep Your Vibration High

Keep your vibration high
That's what you told me
The day that he left me
Smile and wish him 'goodbye'
Let go full of good grace
No tears and no sad face
Smile
It's not worthwhile
To waste tears if he don't care
Be strong
It won't be long
Before your real love is here

Time to love yourself more
You must be your best friend
To make all those tears end
You'll find a love for sure
Next time you'll be stronger
Won't take it no longer
Oh
I think you know
You know he'll never return
Oh
Why is it so
It takes us so long to learn?

HR Meeting

Thanks for coming in today
We have something to say
This probation's not going too well
Such unfortunate errors
Have created some terrors
All around it creates a bad smell

Colleagues have been debating
And the fuss it's creating
Means they're failing to keep on their task
Let's call this one a warning
And we'll meet in the morning
Competence isn't too much to ask

Productive

Economic growth requires inequality
Those without must work hard to get more
Ensure salaries are many times greater
Between boardroom and the lowly shopfloor

Instruct our children in the cult of productivity
Let not minutes be wasted in vain
Each day dedicated to profit and output
Relaxation a beast to be slain

No idle slow living in this nation of doers
Keep them used to the graft and the grind
And when Earth's rich resources have been blasted and burnt up
There'll be other living planets to find

The Other Black Door

The other black door
Near Westminster's lanes
Issues think tank reports
Hoping donors make gains

Pushes privatisation
Reduced role for the state
Finds its views in the Acts
It has helped to create

Fringe views changed to mainstream
Hard to know who's behind
But its young alumni
See their papers refined

Into radio reports
Popular interviews
Making sure narratives
Find their way to the news

Meanwhile friends in the House
Announce they'll stop the rot
Hope the other back door
Will for now be forgot

Serious Disruption

How do we interpret
'Serious Disruption'?
Let's make it ambiguous
Meaning any interruption

Could become a reason why
We remove a person who
Disagrees with how we think
Anything we say is true

Then too late we realise
Once strong laws now frail and weak
When they smile and tell us how
They've removed our right to speak

Feedback

Thanks a lot for the feedback
On my first wobbly days
Didn't expect
You'd reject
So much I had to say

Hope you'll let me stay on
As my office is nice
Learned the lessons
First impressions
Rarely get given twice

One more thing while we're here
About me you will find
A predilection
An affliction
Often changing my mind

Wasn't firmly discussed
As we talked contract terms
I'll still make
More mistakes
As my Comms still confirms

A Break in the Law

The Rule of Law is for everyone
Not just for the small
Or those without money
Applying to all

It's a golden thread weaved through
A compass to guide
Not a nuisance or challenge
When agendas collide

It's a promise to each citizen
That their country is fair
No one better or lesser
It applies everywhere

If there's risk it is threatened
As it sometimes may be
That's the time it's defended
Fierce supporters will plea

Then there may be discussion
It's not needed at all
And those worried it's dying
Shouldn't worry at all

But once lost it is missed
Like the sun or fresh air
Suddenly there's a fear
That the state doesn't care

Spinning

Okay ya
The Comms were off ha
More focus groups
Might have been wise
We frightened the horses
By going off courses
Mortgage holders
Began to despise

When they read in the press
News too hard to digest
They blamed us
Which we think was unfair
Next time we'll do more prep
Avoid such a mis-step
Avoid rumours like cuts
To welfare

It's the right thing to do
When a plan's fallen through
If caught out
By your own ignorance
May we meekly suggest
We did this as a test
As we plead you give us
One more chance

We've had so little training
Any respect remaining
We can see falling
Just like the pound
Let us get back on track
Yes we still have your back
Hang on tight while
We turn this around

Advocate Not Required

In the systems we make
It is well understood
People feel powerless
Statutes state that they should

Have an advocate where
Human rights are maintained
If within social care
Child in need or detained

But too few see these rights
Other people decide
What is best in their life
Justice often denied

No one should have the right
Once these rights are acquired
To state in someone's notes
Advocate not required

No Idea

Ideologies need their proponents
And proponents must be paid
Public speakers need deposits
At the time a booking's made

For there's always someone willing
If of course the price is right
With a menu listing favours
Cheapest offer flying kites

Testing water checking feedback
Laying ground for new ideas
Moves the dial a little further
All the while allaying fears

When suggestions once outrageous
Now appear solutions to
Problems no one else saw coming
But they're lucky they've got you

To declare there is an answer
Well researched and watertight
Benefitting all impacted
Though we might change overnight

Soon the targeted donations
Are investments made worthwhile
Gain respect among the mainstream
It's their slogan but your smile

No Idea cont.

Poverty a chosen lifestyle
Laziness a preference
Poor choices, indecision
Though its hard and makes no sense

Inequality has purpose
Think it should be reappraised
As a tool to serve a system
Not a scourge to be erased

Policies without a mandate
Are presented now as fact
Manifestos urge a small state
Only markets can react

Darwen Street Plaque

The textile mill workers
Said they'd had enough
Of working conditions
Making family life tough

Organised in a pub
To extinguish the heat
Of the factory boilers
Walking up Darwen Street

Met the national army
Who were quick to react
Only pausing to read out
The State's Riot Act

Five men were deported
Where they worked till their grave
Now a plaque honours workers
Courageous and brave

What I Wanted

And what I wanted
Well I don't want anymore
What I aspired to
Well now I just abhor
Things in the past that mattered
Left my heart broke and shattered
I found some new things to adore

You can take the gold box back
I don't want that from now on
And the gowns I used to wear
I'll be glad when they're all gone
You can keep the limousine
With the velvet cushioned seats
Tell the driver he can give it
To the family down the street

And the penthouse in the sky
Near the restaurant where we met
I'm handing back the keys
And I'm sure I won't regret
Last of all the diamond ring
When you asked me would we wed
I'll just leave it on the side
You'll remember what I said

Economic Arguments

The gold comes in and the gold goes out
Through centuries in power
Suggestions made to split maybe
By leaders of the hour

A scapegoat or a problem child?
The cheques not always signed
Its economic arguments
Cannot be undermined

Who works within its corridors?
How does a role get hired?
But if a forecast states decline
There's risk you're getting fired

The First Lord back in power now
Attackers don't last long
They try to blame the market
But the market's never wrong

Before the Morning Light

The first time you would let me know
Confessed that you could not say 'No'
She was your siren with a spell
And afterwards you had to tell

I wonder 'do you think to when?'
I wonder 'will I hear again?'
Your love affairs in late night calls
Of heartbreaks and your frequent falls

The third one caught you off your guard
Could not resist though you tried hard
And once again to ease your pain
You let me know your villain's name

The fifth encountered with surprise
You'd never known her deepest eyes
A knowing smile was all it took
Intoxicated with one look

I just can't help it
When they come around
I just can't help it
When I'm feeling found
I need their touch
When I'm alone at night
I say Goodbye
Before the morning
Say Goodbye
Before the morning
Say Goodbye
Before the morning light

A Paradigm Spell

In offices and wards
The paradigm spell
Casts its shadow throughout
But if you're not well

Or a loved one's in danger
And you're screaming their pain
Those under the spell
State over again

That only their way
Is the right road to take
It's a linear path
That creates no mistake

Don't muddy the water
Or make them think twice
They're the experts, not you
And they won't take advice

But the spell can be broken
With a different view
With the magical words
'Let's listen to you'

Targets

Now you're on the team
We're sure you'll get on
Targets must be achieved
To be sure you're not gone

You'll soon be aware
It's competitive here
Find a mentor to guide
They're your friend never fear

Make sure to be visible
If your aim is the top
Blending in not advised
Not committed? Then stop

Now's your time to show us
Our success is your goal
Salary small reward
In return for your soul

Expectations are high
We expect you to meet
Put the hours in you might
Make it to the C-Suite

Every hour give your best
No room for small mistakes
We'll appraise effort by
All the profits you make

Agency

The woman at the desk
Was mugged for her agency
Enabled to cage
Excused for the urgency

With each passing day
Her memory recedes
Until she forgets
To ask for her needs

No one will speak up
When she no longer knows
Others making decisions
When her speech starts to slow

Stolen gifts now returned
Vows she'll never let go
Those who mugged her before
Claim they just didn't know

Ignorance, Overwhelm and Arrogance

When Ignorance met Overwhelm
And Arrogance came by
The woman sat in front of them
So pained she felt she'd die

No lesson in the training of
The three friends in the schooling
Meant every time she spoke to them
She heard them overruling

Despite their role in caring for her
Just the same as men
She felt the cold dismissal from them
Time and time again

But that was many years ago
Now Understanding's hired
And Ignorance, Arrogance and Overwhelm?
Those three friends

They got fired

How to Talk To Your Child About the Cost-of-Living Crisis

Today within our phone-in show
The subject on the air
Is how to tell a five-year old
That money's all too rare

Our experts tell us helpfully
How you can get it right
When little ones who fear the dark
Must wash without a light

Or when they're cold and shivering
Turn challenges to fun
Just get them running on the spot
That should heat everyone

If shoes are tight then make them stretch
Or cut them at the end
So toes peek out into fresh air
It could become a trend

But listeners in all seriousness
Our experts do agree
Your child will need to understand
Harsh inequality

Perhaps it might be only when
This new young generation
Are adults that we finally see
A fairer equal nation

Still Standing But Wobbling Part Two

Still standing but wobbling
Over serious matters
But colleagues risk seeing
Reputations in tatters

Warn they'll lose their careers
Facing certain defeat
While it's hoped they stay loyal
More and more in retreat

Let me stick with my dream
Let me grow this damn pie
Okay someone messed up
Can I have one more try?

When we wrote on the page
We'd force change we'd disrupt
Never thought it would end
Such a mess so corrupt

It's not true when you say
Our experiment's failed
And the dreams families planned
Thrown off course now derailed

I must do as I'm told
State this one point of view
And I'll not be content
Till I've seen this job through

Built on Trust

Trust arrives at a snail's pace
And leaves on a jet
When the building explodes
There is rubble and yet

There's still the old bricks
Left behind whole intact
Just a few but enough
To begin building back

Locks from windows and doors
Blown to dust now need new
Sharpened edges of glass
Nothing more to see through

So the bricklayer tries
With the few tools to make
Calls the locksmith within
Hopes the new locks can't break

And a new home emerges
Solid windows and doors
Have replaced what was old
To protect her once more

The Alternative Economic Advisory Council

The volunteer at the foodbank
Sending out requests to say
Once again the shelves look empty
Hates to turn people away
Asking neighbours can they bring in
Dried food, loo roll and toothpaste
Sanitary products too please
No donation goes to waste

And the teacher paying for things
From her own purse for her class
After months of asking parents
This time seems too much to ask
Basics like the pens and pencils
Children need these every day
But the school budget is shrinking
No it can't afford to pay

Next the debt advisor hearing
That his client on the call
Is now facing repossession
Mortgage can't be paid at all
Has been decided that the best choice
Faced with rising interest debt
Is to hand the keys back hoping
Credit agencies forget

Then the shop owner despairing
As the income line descends
Customers have just stopped buying
Hopes to turn round worrying trends
Still keeps going optimistic
The next quarter will go well
Otherwise she'll shut for good and
Have no option but to sell

Courtroom Drama

We took a ferry to the court
I said I'd stick around
To help you find your smile again
I knew it could be found

You said you felt a real despair
From others felt betrayed
Unfairly judged they slammed the door
On future plans you'd made

They showed no mercy though they could
Imposing rules instead
The coming drama on a loop
Continued in your head

I said 'you must keep going on'
And stuck by you despite
My own place in the dock alone
I knew I had to. Right?

Workplace Politics

How you get things done
Is nothing to do with
If you got an A
Or even a C
Though where you
Acquired them could
Come in handy
If told correctly

It's all about alliances
And allegiances
Your ideas are
Merely policies
If they don't like you
They won't like
Your ideas
Either

It's not always
A bad thing
Some ideas are
Actually good
But they still
Require
A little
Encouragement

Preparing for
Meetings is key
Know who will
Advocate for you
When you're
Not in the room
Or unable to attend
The Church Committee

Psychographics

We're interested in your habits
These will give us handy clues
Let us build a complete picture
So we really can know you

All your future aspirations
By next year where will you be?
Let us help you with your choices
See your profile more clearly

What opinions are you holding?
What's your favourite type of food
Monday morning? What you doing?
We have products for your mood

What's your go-to when you're tired?
How would friends describe your style?
Every hint you keep on dropping
We'll upload to your profile

Every breadcrumb that you leave us
We'll pick up to know you well
That's the reason you keep buying
And the reason we can sell

What's your attitude to ageing
Your concerns regarding health?
If unsure ask us we're sure to
Know you better than yourself

Verify You're Not a Robot

Verify you're not a robot
Tick the heartbeats on the grid
If there's none then you can press 'skip'
Then again they could be hid

Can you verbalise a sentence?
That at least sounds you are here?
Verify you're not a robot
Your responses induce fear

Just repeating the same wording
Never mind the questions asked
Give impressions you're a robot
Or at least not up to task

Your Story is Your Strength

Your story is your   Strength
But you'll go to any   Length
Not to tell it

Someone else's and you're   Fine
Your own you're less   Inclined
No doubt about it

The darkness and the   Shade
The part of you that   Made
The light shine from you

Such beauty deep   Inside
So there's no need to   Hide
The brightness in you

Gendered Emotions

She is
Completely hysterical
Uncontrolled in a state
Fanatical hormonal
Shes probably late
Influenced by the misfortune
Of her biological fate
Don't take her too seriously
She'll only create

He on the other hand
Is angry because
He's spent too much money
Or his team's gone and lost
Entirely justified
He's a rational male
Just as long as he's careful
He won't end up in jail

She on the other hand
Needs to keep it all in
Stay calm in a crisis
Though she still may not win
Taught that anger won't do
If she's wanting affection
Hysterical women always
Deserved their rejection

When We're Given a Choice

I wish you a life
No longer in pain
For how can two humans
Think either will gain?
Perhaps it was grief
Which held you in fear
Or loss made you run
When love came too near

Or numbed by some coldness
Thought no other way
Not trusting another
You faced every day
Do we really want life
In a world which can't feel
When we're given the choice
To create one that heals?

Going to Thrive

Thrive was a country
Far from Survival
A different place
From its opposite rival

A recent discovery
She'd found on a map
Almost discarded
After another mishap

But its colours looked vibrant
Its mountains so high
In the midst of a sea
Underneath its own sky

From the port in Survival
She set off for its shore
No idea of the voyage
Hadn't been there before

Only setting her compass
Hoped at last she'd arrive
Knew she couldn't go wrong
And continued to Thrive

Protest at the Panto

There's a protest at the Panto
Saying no man in a dress
Should be entertaining children
And the country's in a mess
It's not right that men in make-up
Should tell stories to the young
And that children shouldn't see them
When they're obviously wrong

They are angered that these 'ladies'
Are allowed upon the stage
Making risky innuendos
And that's why they're so enraged
Where might all this madness take us?
State the protestors in fear
Pantos are no place for children
Panto dames aren't welcome here

Unique is My Path

Unique is my path in unfolding
No other will walk the same way
Each view I take in while beholding
The progress I make every day

For each must respond to their calling
And make the steep climb till they see
The view from the top of their mountain
To say then at last they are free

Words in Ink

Everything she knows she writes it down
Throwing big emotions in the sound
Making meaning with the letters
Makes her feel a little better

On the page her words in ink
Tells her how she's gonna think
Carves an epic from the stone
Now she won't feel so alone
And she's a storyteller now
She's a storyteller now
She never thought she'd be a storyteller
Never thought she'd be a storyteller
But she's a storyteller now

Once upon a lifetime let's begin
She opened up her heart to let him in
She'd never read the book how could she know
Soon he would become her brave hero

On the page her words in ink
Tells her how she's gonna think
Carves an epic from the stone
Now she won't feel so alone
And she's a storyteller now
She's a storyteller now
She never thought she'd be a storyteller
Never thought she'd be a storyteller
But she's a storyteller now

Words in Ink cont.

The chapter ends with a twist in plot
A fairytale all too soon forgot
It's only now that she understands
Don't leave the last page in his hands

On the page my words in ink
Tells me how I'm gonna think
Carved an epic from the stone
Now I won't feel so alone
And I'm a storyteller now
I'm a storyteller now
I never thought I'd be a storyteller
Never thought I'd be a storyteller
But I'm a storyteller now

www.ingramcontent.com/pod-product-compliance
Lightning Source LLC
Chambersburg PA
CBHW030044100526
44590CB00011B/332